Okendo Lewis-Gayle
Harambeans

OKENDO LEWIS-GAYLE is founder and chairman of the Harambe Entrepreneur Alliance (HEA) – a network of highly educated young African entrepreneurial leaders, who, as signatories of the Harambe Bretton Woods Declaration, are committed: *to work together as one to unleash the potential of Africa's people... and fulfill the dream of our generation.* These young leaders, known as Harambeans, are translating the lofty principles of the Harambe Declaration into the concrete gains of their social and business ventures across Africa – efforts which have been recognized by the Economist, Forbes, Vanity Fair, China Daily and the Queen of England among others.

Starting in 2007, in partnership with Fortune 500 companies and Ivy League universities, Okendo has overseen the development of HEA's diverse ecosystem of opportunities aimed at supporting the entrepreneurial aspirations of young African professionals with mentors, feasibility study grants, scholarships, pro bono legal services and access to angel and venture capital.

For nearly a decade, Okendo has interacted with African professionals in over 30 campuses around the world and worked closely with the over 200 Harambeans, who represent 33 African countries and are graduates of leading universities in Africa, Asia, Europe and North America, institutions such as Harvard, HEC Paris, Oxford, Stanford, Tsinghua, and the University of Cape Town.

Okendo is part of Africa's historical diaspora – the over 12 million Africans who were shipped to the Americas during the Transatlantic Slave Trade. Born in Costa Rica, raised in Italy, and educated in the United States and Taiwan, Okendo has recently been admitted to the Harvard Kennedy School to continue his master's studies as a member of the prestigious Edward S. Mason Program.

HARAMBEANS

Ordinary People Doing
Extraordinary Things

———

Okendo Lewis-Gayle

HARAMBE BRETTON WOODS PRESS

Alla mia bellissima mamma, Cecilia Gayle.

To the gracious co-authors and contributors
of our *Dream on a Piece of Paper.*

To the young entrepreneurial leaders across the Continent
yearning for a peaceful, prosperous and equitable Africa.

CONTENTS

FOREWORD

I came across the Harambe Entrepreneur Alliance in my first meeting with Okendo at the World Bank in 2007. Since then, I have seen his perseverance transform an idea into a global institution, which today supports the ambitions of young entrepreneurs across Africa with scholarships, fellowships, angel investors and a growing number of opportunities.

I have visited the companies and interacted with Harambeans in Nigeria such as Obinna Ukwuani, Oluseun Onigbinde and Iyinoluwa Aboyeji. Young Nigerians who are putting the admirable commitments of the Harambe Bretton Woods Declaration into practice with their exemplary ventures in education (Makers Academy), governance (BudgIT) and technology (Andela), respectively.

I have experienced the power of the collective example of Harambeans to inspire other young Africans to act on their dreams and embolden prestigious universities, African governments and multinational corporations to rally around the Alliance. Yet, as Okendo argues, it all begins with ordinary people choosing to do extraordinary things.

Okendo's brief and timely reflection affords us insights into the character and innovative potential of Africa's youth. I hope you will enjoy it as much as I have enjoyed watching the steady progress of Harambe. May it inspire other young Africans and strengthen our confidence in the unlimited potential of Africa's youth.

Obiageli Ezekwesili
World Bank Africa Vice President (2007–2012)
Minister of Education, Nigeria (2006–2007)

INTRODUCTION

We publish and declare our intention to work together as one
to unleash the potential of Africa's people, pursue the social, political
and economic development of our Continent and fulfill
the dream of our generation.

This was the solemn pledge made by Olivia Mukam, HEA '08, on the hopeful spring day of April 19, 2008, in the Gold Room of the historic Mount Washington Hotel, 64 years after the winning powers of World War II assembled in the same room to sign the Bretton Woods Agreements – accords which gave rise to the World Bank and the International Monetary Fund.

Bretton Woods was a far distance from Ms. Mukam's native Cameroon. Yet, the challenges and opportunities of her country were at the forefront of her mind as she, and 31 other enterprising young Africans, gathered in the Gold Room to sign the Harambe Bretton Woods Declaration.

Representing 13 African countries and 21 prestigious universities from across North America, the energy of the group mirrored the growing optimism of a Continent that was transitioning from the narrative of a *Hopeless Continent* to one of *Africa Rising*, an unfolding tale of transformation which *The Economist* magazine memorably profiled in 2000 and 2011 respectively.

One by one, Ms. Mukam and her fellow Harambeans in the Gold Room, took turns at the rosewood table to sign the Harambe Bretton Woods Declaration. A profound ritual which has been observed every April since then by successive classes of the Harambe Entrepreneur Alliance.

"In July 2009, inspired by MIT's $100k business plan competition," recalled a jovial Ms. Mukam, "I decided to go back home to launch Harambe Cameroon, an entrepreneurship program which I hoped would enable the youth to transform our challenges into opportunities."

The move back to Cameroon, which came at the conclusion of her studies at Johns Hopkins University, worried Ms. Mukam's friends and family. "Some of my friends were so puzzled by my decision to leave the U.S. that they became convinced I was being deported." Richard, a former primary school classmate who had also attended college in the United States and had since fully integrated into American society, suggested that Ms. Mukam was being too optimistic. He warned that the pervasive corruption, hidebound bureaucracy and inadequate infrastructure in Cameroon would impede the realization of her initiative. Her brother, Christian Mukam, was also perplexed. Whenever she would start to enthusiastically explain the concept of Harambe Cameroon to others he would joke in French "*Elle te Harambefie,*" she is Harambefying you.

In spite of the objections, Ms. Mukam was so determined to return to Cameroon that she opted to finish her studies at Johns Hopkins University six months early, and decided to forgo an opportunity to work in the United States. Her father, a construction engineer who had risen from extreme poverty, had taught her to always respect and help the least fortunate around her. As a child, he would also take her to his construction sites where she watched in awe as vast tracts of empty land were transformed into hospitals, schools and banks. "My father's genuine care for others and his ability to erect concrete structures from detailed architectural drawings," Ms. Mukam contended, "is probably why I've always thought it was my responsibility to leverage my own skills to help develop the country. It also probably explains why I never doubted that my well-thought-out plans would eventually blossom into Cameroon's own version of MIT's $100k. So for me, going back was a simple and obvious decision, and I just couldn't understand why others didn't see it that way."

Yet when the ebullient Ms. Mukam returned home, she soon realized that the concerns of her loved ones were not only well grounded, but, as she put it, "an underestimation of the challenges I ultimately faced." Beyond the issues that her friends had predicted, Ms. Mukam also dealt with sexism, theft and mistrust. "I now completely understand," she remarked, "why some people give up."

As she contemplated surrender, Ms. Mukam asked herself, "if not I, then who? If I, fortunate enough to have access to opportunities, networks and education – if I give up, then how will the situation in Cameroon ever change? I would be partly responsible for the status quo and my complaints about the system would probably fall on deaf ears." In those trying moments, Ms. Mukam revealed, "the promise of our Declaration kept me going: *Yet in the end, the Africa our generation desires, can be won, it exists, it is real, it is possible, it is ours.*"

Ms. Mukam has not given up. Her servant leadership, enduring optimism and deliberate audacity have enabled Harambe Cameroon to blossom into a nationwide business plan competition. The program has trained over 1,200 young Cameroonians: entrepreneurial leaders in the mold of Mr. Alain Nteff, founder of GiftedMom, a mobile-based solution aimed at improving the health practices of pregnant women in rural areas, which has received funding from investors in the United States and South Africa. In July 2015, exactly six years after Ms. Mukam's return, Mr. Nteff's efforts to transform Cameroon's challenges into opportunities were honored by the Queen of England at a ceremony in Buckingham Palace.

Yet, what has been even more rewarding for Ms. Mukam is that her example has inspired others to act. Richard, her former classmate, emboldened by her work in Cameroon decided to move back home to start a venture of his own and support an entrepreneurship program. Even her perplexed brother, Christian Mukam, was so touched by an exchange in a remote village in southern Cameroon, that on June 14, 2015, he chose to tell his sister, "I have seen the impact of your work through the grateful eyes and testimonies of friends I met in the village. I finally understand what you do. Please keep doing it. The whole country needs to be Harambefied."

As the founder and chairman of the Harambe Entrepreneur Alliance (HEA), I have been privileged to observe Ms. Mukam, now Mrs. Mukam-Wandji, and her fellow Harambeans persevere through the vicissitudes of the new-venture-formation process and translate the lofty principles of our Declaration into the concrete gains of their social and business ventures across Africa.

Over the course of this uplifting process, I've come to appreciate that these ventures are far more than just proposed solutions, but the manifestation of a core set of deeply-rooted values. While the ventures may bend to the inescapable whims of the entrepreneurial process, these values will endure and find expression in the lifelong efforts of these young leaders.

These values are essential to the attainment of broad-based and inclusive prosperity across Africa, for they will shape the solutions that these leaders advance to address the *how* of Africa's development:

- How will Africa propel its burgeoning youth bulge to become an engine of economic growth and not fuel of paralyzing social and political instability?

- How will it structure its rapidly expanding cities to evolve into hubs of innovation and productivity, and not degenerate into centers of wanton violence and abject poverty?

- How will it develop its fertile lands into a prolific source of rural prosperity and balanced economic growth, and not decay into an unsavory compost of speculative investments and displacement of local communities?

- How, in essence, will Africa seize the unprecedented convergence of resources and opportunity to create inclusive social, political and economic gains for all its people?

The strength and authenticity of the values I've observed in the young Africans in our Alliance underpin my conviction that Africa's entrepreneurial leaders have the capacity to formulate suitable answers to these challenging questions. Innovative solutions that could set Africa on an exhilarating course towards shared prosperity.

This brief reflection is a humble attempt to distill my nascent insights on the values propelling the young African innovators whom I've come to know, and to share their journeys with aspiring entrepreneurial leaders across the Continent and enlightened friends of Africa around the world. It harbors no ambition of being a comprehensive compendium on African entrepreneurship. It simply seeks to capture the edifying stories that inform my evolving understanding of the role these values can play in our collective quest for a prosperous Africa. I hope to foster further study into the subject and inject it into the ongoing discussion of youth entrepreneurship across the Continent.

In the interest of brevity, I've chosen to shed light on the stories of three Harambeans: Kwami Williams, HEA '14, Sabina Ndakorerwa, HEA '10, and Obinna Ukwuani, HEA '09. These individuals respectively elucidate my understanding of three salient traits of values-driven leaders like Mrs. Mukam-Wandji: Servant Leadership, Enduring Optimism and Deliberate Audacity. I conclude this reflection with an overview of the collective journey of our *Dream on a Piece of Paper*, as we fondly refer to the Alliance.

Throughout the narrative, you will notice my penchant to refer to Harambeans by their surnames. It reflects Harambe's decade-old culture of professionalism and serves as a daily reminder that our Declaration commitments have not yet been fulfilled.

In the spirit of Chinua Achebe's assertion that "until the lions have their own historians, tales of the hunt will always glorify the hunters," it is my hope that this reflection will accelerate the glorification of Africa's young entrepreneurial leaders as the heroic lions in the emerging tale of *Africa Rising*. They are the innovators that will answer the *how* of Africa's development. They represent our best hope to unlock Africa's potential in the 21st century, and as such they are deserving of our wholehearted support and genuine admiration.

As the first decade with Harambe draws near, it is perhaps only natural that Harambeans are the protagonists of my exploration. These are the 108 women and 108 men, representing 33 African countries, who make up our Alliance to date, and are driving change within influential organizations or through their own social and business ventures. Together, we have transformed "a rickety idea in a turbulent sea of skepticism" into a global institution, which supports the entrepreneurial aspirations of young African leaders with scholarships, feasibility study grants, mentors, pro bono legal services and access to angel and venture capital.

Along the way, Harambeans have earned the admiration of their peers, as reflected in the thousands of applications to our Alliance each year, while prominent figures and reputable organizations across Africa and around the world continue to lend their names and support to our Alliance, from the Parliaments of Ghana and South Africa, to Yale University, Vanity Fair and the Vatican.

While the stories of the young Africans in our Alliance are my focus, the traits and values they exemplify are not unique to Harambeans. For as my global campus recruitment sessions remind me each year, these traits and values appear to be shared among young Africans with a bias towards action, those who, as our Declaration states, are: *cognizant of the daunting challenges that face a Continent. Yet, eager to take their turn at Africa's helm.*

Perhaps the only truly distinctive trait of Harambeans is their declared choice to accept their individual responsibility in the realization of Africa's potential. A responsibility they publicly assume as signatories of the Harambe Bretton Woods Declaration:

We therefore, sons and daughters of Africa, assembled in the Harambe Entrepreneur Alliance, with the assistance of those who have come before us and those who share our vision, publish and declare our intention to work together as one to unleash the potential of Africa's people, pursue the social, political and economic development of our Continent and fulfill the dream of our generation.

Yet, as the example of Richard in Cameroon reminds us, this choice is ultimately available to all young Africans across the Continent and around the world. For Harambeans are simply ordinary people doing extraordinary things. Individuals who, in spite of their fears, shortcomings and obstacles, have chosen to play a role in the advancement of their communities. They are products of our time, excited about the prospect to leapfrog development across Africa, yet conscious of the daunting challenges ahead. What makes their effort extraordinary is not just impact, growth or commercial success, but like Mrs. Mukam-Wandji's journey demonstrates, it is their deliberate choice to be active participants in the design of the future of their countries.

I believe that this deliberate choice is indispensable to the realization of the Continent's potential. For while Africa's current economic trend is propitious, trend is not destiny. To secure lasting gains from the current momentum, more young Africans must choose to be active participants and help establish the plurality of efforts that will in time deliver suitable answers to the *how* of Africa's development.

Quoting Marianne Williamson, President Nelson Mandela once noted that "as we let our light shine, we unconsciously give other people permission to do the same." In this spirit, it is my sincere hope that as Mrs. Mukam-Wandji inspired Richard, the stories and choices of the Harambeans in this brief reflection will inspire other young Africans to embrace the commitments of the Harambe Bretton Woods Declaration and embolden us all to become active participants in the pursuit of a peaceful, prosperous and equitable Africa.

CHAPTER I

Servant Leadership
Kwami Williams, HEA '14

"I was sitting with a group of five students at Tamale Polytechnic in northern Ghana" recalls Mr. Kwami Williams, HEA '14. "I was walking them through their curiosities about the Bible. I was telling them: 'this is who God is. This is how he loves you. This is how you can build a relationship with him.' After almost three hours, a distant clatter of forks and knives challenged me to ask, 'Have you guys eaten today? Are you going to eat?' 'No,' they said. 'No food today.' It suddenly struck me that these were students who were likely eating one meal a day at most. Yet, I was heading back to a warm meal in the volunteer camp. At the end of the summer, I went back to the U.S. to start my junior year as an aerospace engineering major at MIT. But I just couldn't let go of my experience at Tamale Polytechnic. Challenging verses in the Bible kept coming to mind: *I was hungry and you gave me something to eat, I was naked and you clothed me. I was sick and you visited me. I was in prison and you came to me.* These passages helped me crystallize the disconnect between what my faith professed and how I was actually living. I realized that I couldn't let this kind of poverty, this kind of destruction, this kind of hunger last another 50 years, if I could do something about it now. I abandoned my plans to go to NASA after graduation, and began to explore ways to leverage my time at MIT to address the needs of the people in the villages and communities I'd visited that summer."

Upon graduation in 2012, the tall Ghanaian with a beaming smile returned to his native country to lay the foundation for what is now MoringaConnect – an agribusiness venture which provides training, inputs, and income to smallholder farmers growing the Moringa tree in Ghana and turns their harvested seeds into a cosmetic oil and the leaves into a micronutrient powder sold in Ghana and the United States. Since its incorporation in 2013, the venture has scaled to over 1,000 farmers and planted 250,000 Moringa trees in each of Ghana's ten regions.

Mr. Williams exemplifies my most consistent observation of the young Africans who have signed the Harambe Bretton Woods Declaration: a wholehearted commitment to servant leadership. Demonstrated by Harambeans in unique ways, servant leadership, at its core, is a desire to put their skills, networks, and education at the service of their communities. It is an admirable willingness to make the sacrifices necessary to unlock Africa's potential, an instinctive embrace of the principle that to whom much is given, much is expected in return.

Like many of his fellow Harambeans, Mr. Williams traces the roots of his servant leadership to the example set by his parents. "My parents have a huge heart for people. It was never just about my brother and me. They were always caring for someone else's kids or someone else's family. They taught us that once you are connected to someone else's problems, you have a responsibility to try to solve them." This was a lesson that was further and forever etched on Mr. Williams' mind, following the death of his uncle. "My mom's younger sister lost her husband shortly after the birth of their second child. He was accidentally killed by a police officer who shot into an open market in pursuit of a burglar. The bullet ricocheted off a wall and fatally wounded my uncle, while he was buying baby food for their newborn baby. It was a devastating blow. As is customary in Ghana, the extended family rallied around my aunt. However, at the end of the grieving period, most drifted away with the expectation that my aunt would fend for herself. My parents didn't. They purchased land, built a home, and created job opportunities for my aunt. They adopted two of her children and helped them immigrate to the U.S. where they moved in with us and became full members of our family."

In line with the background of many Harambeans, Mr. Williams hails from humble beginnings. Born on August 20, 1991, in Accra, Ghana, he is the youngest of two children. His mother was one of ten and had to help raise her two younger siblings following the death of her father. Mr. Williams explains, "My mom went from only caring about going to school to managing the household. In a way, she was forced to become an entrepreneur at a very early age. She sold candy, snacks and salads at school to pay for her school fees and, ultimately, the fees of her two younger siblings." In contrast, Mr. Williams' father lived the first part of his life in a middle-income home. However, by the age of seven, the fortunes of his family changed and "as the oldest of all the children, Dad had to start finding creative ways to support the family."

In 2000, Mr. Williams' parents won a visa to immigrate to the United States. It was a bittersweet victory as it triggered an abrupt end to their lives in Ghana and a start from scratch in the U.S. The U.S. did not recognize the Ghanaian education and work experience of his parents, so they worked menial jobs and went back to school with students who were often twenty or thirty years younger. Nevertheless, they accepted the sacrifices moving to America entailed for the sake of securing quality education and better career opportunities for their two boys. "It happened. My brother has a master's in construction management and is managing MIT's Lincoln Lab facilities, while I got to pursue my father's passion for aviation at MIT and even intern at NASA. In a way, we lived out a lot of their immigrant dreams. It just came at a much, much higher cost."

Ten years after his family's move to the United States, Mr. Williams seized an opportunity to volunteer with a Christian organization and return to Ghana for the first time in June 2010. "Suddenly Ghana became alive again. It wasn't just occasional hellos over the phone with relatives. But now the people, the culture, the music, the food, it was all real again." It was during this visit that Mr. Williams met with the five students at Tamale Polytechnic. The discussion had such an impact on him that by the start of his junior year at MIT, his priorities had changed. "Junior year was war. I would be in my aerodynamics class and think 'this is cool, this is amazing, but it doesn't do anything for what I just experienced in Ghana.' This bug, this itch, ultimately forced me to stop thinking so much about sexy propulsion engines and focus, instead, on sustainable solutions for the people back home."

Thus, Mr. Williams embarked on a two-year-long search that, ultimately, led him to the Moringa fields of Ghana. He added a concentration in global development to his studies and in January 2011, traveled back to Ghana with a program of MIT's D-Lab. It was then that he connected with the challenges of Moringa farmers, who were living on less than $2 a day, and learned of the untapped potential of Moringa trees. "I met smallholder farmers who kept telling us that they had an oversupply of Moringa trees in their backyards. Aid organizations advised them to eat the leaves to fight malnutrition, but they couldn't make a living from the trees and were throwing away the seeds. They wanted us to help. I didn't know how, but I knew I had to try. Fortunately, I wasn't alone. Through my global development classes I met my co-founder, Emily Cunningham. Emily was studying economics at Harvard, but like me she was craving for a more practical application of her knowledge and had joined our trip to Ghana. Together we discovered why farmers called Moringa the miracle tree. Gram for gram, the leaves contain more vitamin A than carrots, more vitamin C than oranges, more iron than spinach, more calcium than milk, and more protein than eggs. The seeds, rich in antioxidants and moisturizing agents, produce one of nature's finest oils for hair and skin care. Even the oil processing waste could be used as an organic fertilizer, animal feed, and flocculant to purify water. So when the farmers asked us to help them figure out a way earn a living from Moringa trees we were excited." Enabled by funding from MIT's D-Lab, Mr. Williams leveraged his engineering skills to develop proprietary Moringa processing technologies, while Emily used her business insights to identify the market opportunities. "Together," he noted, "we developed MoringaConnect's vertically-integrated supply chain that today helps farmers capture the nutrition and income trapped in their Moringa trees and gives consumers the chance to connect with our social impact and enjoy the benefits of our products."

I caught up with Mr. Williams on June 12, 2015 in Zurich, Switzerland. He was participating in a Harambe *friend-raising* dinner organized by the former CEO of Deutsche Telekom and attended by the former President of Switzerland along with several Swiss-based investors. During our wide-ranging interview, Mr. Williams came to the pleasant realization that quite inadvertently, the majority of his network of smallholder farmers were based in and around Tamale. The same region which ultimately ignited his desire to serve Ghana's Moringa farmers.

The desire to leverage skills to create scalable solutions is another defining characteristic of the servant leadership I have observed. For Mr. Williams and his fellow Harambeans, servant leadership is about more than just helping others. It is also about choice, skills and scale. "Ultimately, I, and people of similar backgrounds, are in a position to pursue more immediately lucrative opportunities. But instead, we choose to leverage our global networks, our acquired skills, our blessings to develop not just well-intentioned, feel-good solutions but systemic and sustainable ones. Solutions that are influenced by all the opportunities that have molded us professionally. Opportunities which we could use to help corporations make a lot more money, but instead leverage to change individual lives, families, rural communities."

The depth of the commitment to servant leadership by Mr. Williams and his fellow Harambeans can be inferred from the hard choices and sacrifices they stand ready to make. "When I told my parents that I would not continue my career track to NASA, but would instead head back to Ghana to start a social venture, it was very painful for them. Particularly, for my Mom. She was working two jobs and going to school full-time as a nursing student at the time. No matter how I tried to explain it, all she could hear was – my son is dropping out of MIT and heading back to Ghana to do missionary work. I kept saying 'no, I am going to finish my final year at MIT, graduate, then start a company in Ghana.' I am just not going to pursue a career in aerospace engineering.' But no matter how many times I tried, my message just wasn't getting through. It was an emotional experience. It was tough on Dad, too. I think he was mostly concerned with the evaporation of his aviation dream. Growing up, he was an aviation enthusiast. He would visit libraries to read books about planes, engines and avionics. His passion, ultimately, influenced my choice for aerospace engineering at MIT. So it was difficult for him as well. My parents' concerns then fed into my own worries about the financial repercussions of my choice on the family. It is simply not easy. These are just some of the real challenges that weigh heavily on the minds of social entrepreneurs. I just hope to show them one day that doing good and doing well are not mutually exclusive."

Fortunately, Mr. Williams didn't have to wait long to gain the endorsement of his parents. Once they came to appreciate the impact and promise of MoringaConnect, they became his anchor in the turbulent sea of new venture formation. "I have wanted to give up so many times. Particularly when you are on the ground and you are doing everything you can, but sometimes you feel that the country, the system, the people are not just passively but actively impeding you. People you expect to be supportive wonder 'why are you back in Ghana?' In those trying moments, the prayers and encouragements of my parents have kept me afloat. Once they realized that the farmers I was dealing with weren't just numbers on a World Bank report, but real people with real problems, they understood that I ultimately was doing what they had taught me: solving the problems of people that I was connected to. Dad has spent considerable time in Ghana since I moved back to support me and the MoringaConnect team. From cooking delicious meals to managing the renovation of our processing facility, his support on the ground has been invaluable. Mom and I talk constantly on the phone. It's funny and helpful to see her dust off her entrepreneurial skills and pepper me with questions, often more probing than the ones I get from investors doing due diligence. Costs, revenues, price fluctuations, she wants to know every single detail. She is like my new Chief Financial Officer. My brother, Kofi, has also been incredibly supportive. He keeps my passion for Africa ablaze and has gone out of his way to shoulder the financial burdens of my choice on the family."

Three years on, Mr. Williams' commitment to servant leadership and MoringaConnect remains undiminished. He is currently raising a seed round of investment to scale his operations and find new markets for Moringa products. In July 2015, he was among the Harambeans who were flown to Kenya, by the U.S. State Department, to attend President Obama's Global Entrepreneurship Summit. Among hundreds of entrepreneurs from around the world, five were selected as winners of the Summit's pitch contest. Two of the prizes were awarded to Harambeans, including Mr. Williams, who took the prize back to Ghana and proudly gave his parents his certificate for the African Impact Award.

CHAPTER II

Enduring Optimism
Sabina Ndakorerwa, HEA '10

Listening attentively to the final presentation on the company's strategy in Rwanda in June 2015 were managers of the pharmaceutical giant, GlaxoSmithKline (GSK). Their presenter, 24-year-old Ms. Sabina Ndakorerwa, HEA '10, was advising the group in her role as a Harambe GSK Fellow. "At first, I wondered how on earth such a major company could give me such a huge responsibility. I had the power to hire and set up all focus groups. I conducted probing interviews with Rwandan doctors, pharmacists, and patients. Most had never even been asked for their opinion of pharmaceutical products. I compiled the findings and developed a cohesive narrative about the needs of underserved segments of the population and the benefits GSK could derive from tailoring packaging and product delivery to meet their unique needs. By the end of our discussion, I could tell that I had awakened them to a new opportunity and they were genuinely excited about Rwanda. So eventually I came to realize that in spite of my young age, I was supposed to be there. As a young Rwandan fortunate to receive a global and pan-African education, I had a responsibility to bridge the gap and help portray my country and the needs of my people in a positive light. 'Yes', I thought, 'this is my role."

The moment seemed like a rendezvous with destiny for the petite and thoughtful Ms. Ndakorerwa, born on January 6, 1991, in Hamburg, Germany, to a Rwandan father and a German mother. A self-described corporate intrapreneur, she is among the Harambeans who choose to contribute to the realization of Africa's potential by leveraging their roles within established groups in the private and public sectors. She reminds us of the variety of ways in which we all can be active participants, as long as we choose to try.

Ms. Ndakorerwa has chosen to use her opportunities to infect major health-care companies with her optimism about the future of Rwanda and her Continent. It is an enduring optimism, anchored in a firm vision of a prosperous Africa. It is an optimism that refuses to yield to the overpowering despair of impregnable challenges. It is a flickering flame of hope that consistently outshines the gloomy predictions of critics, skeptics and cynics alike. It is a value that permeates the Harambe Bretton Woods Declaration, which Ms. Ndakorerwa and her fellow Harambeans in the third class of our Alliance signed on April 10, 2010: *We refuse to lose our knowledge that man's proper estate is an upright posture, an intransigent mind and a step that travels unlimited roads…We will not let the hero in our soul perish, in lonely frustration for the life our Continent deserves, but has never been able to reach. We will check our road and the nature of our battle. Yet in the end, the Africa our generation desires can be won, it exists, it is real, it is possible, it is ours.*

"Having lived in Rwanda in the 1990s and seen the enormous progress that the country has made since the Genocide," a reflective Ms. Ndakorerwa noted, "have allowed me to choose optimism. I actually think that optimism is the privilege of our generation. We have seen change. We know that change is possible, so we naturally strive for change. I have seen change in things as basic as a convenience store. When I left Rwanda in 2003, *La Baguette* was one of the only stores in my neighborhood. It was small and prohibitively expensive. It was run and mostly frequented by expats from the U.S. and Europe. But when I returned in 2010, *La Baguette* was dwarfed by the nearby *Nakumatt*, an impressive supermarket chain as big as Walmart. Instead of expats, it was packed with cheerful Rwandan customers, all part of the country's emerging middle class. All in just seven short years."

An optimistic outlook on Rwanda was not an inevitable outcome for the 2010 Harambean. Ms. Ndakorerwa's father experienced the challenges of Rwanda early in life. Political instability in the late 1950s forced his family to flee the country. "At the age of 16, Dad was already working to support his mother and extended family. They left everything behind and lived in precarious conditions as refugees, first in Burundi and then Kenya. Dad doesn't talk much about that experience, but I think it was one of the reasons he consistently stressed the value of education. He viewed it as the key to securing desirable things in life. If my sister and I had to study for an exam, he would make sure we had ample space to focus and spur us on to appreciate it. Curiously, Dad never failed to encourage me to be optimistic and remain engaged in Rwanda. Even though he'd fled the country at a young age and under very difficult circumstances, he is probably one of the most patriotic people I know."

Her father's strong emphasis on education seems to have been a key driver of Ms. Ndakorerwa's global academic achievement. Following her primary and secondary studies in Zambia, Rwanda, and Germany, she attended the Hong Kong University of Science and Technology where she received a bachelor's degree in business administration. In 2013, she became the Harambe Fletcher Scholar, securing a full scholarship to pursue her master's studies at The Fletcher School of Law and Diplomacy.

Ms. Ndakorerwa's optimism is also in contrast with her own childhood memories of Rwanda. "In 1996, my parents moved back to Rwanda. Even though I was only six years old, I definitely remember the tension. It was two years after the Genocide, but tempers were still high. On a few occasions, we came close to being evacuated. There was a constant fear and threat of violence. It was a very difficult time."

Few would fault Ms. Ndakorerwa if her family's experience of Rwanda had hardened into a negative perception of her country and the Continent. But like many of her fellow Harambeans, Ms. Ndakorerwa's enduring optimism is a deliberate choice. A choice she made in a classroom in Germany. "At the age of 13, we moved back to Germany. Even though I'd left Germany at a very young age, I'd always considered myself German. But when I returned to

Germany, it was like a new country to me. I joined the German school system, and as the only person from Rwanda, I quickly became an ambassador, not just for Rwanda, but the whole of Africa. People were just clueless about Africa. The little they knew was coated in a hazy veneer of negativity. Even teachers would ask baffling questions. The question that stuck with me the most came from a geography teacher. He invited me to speak at a class of much older students. In front of the whole class he asked me, 'Many people write that Africa is hopeless. Do you agree?' I must have been 14, but I still remember that question. To him and everyone in that room, it was a foregone conclusion that Africa was hopeless. I thought to myself, 'Gee, I really need to do something. Yes there are difficulties, but there are difficulties in Germany too. Africa is certainly not hopeless.' It had such an impact on me that then and there I decided that I would always highlight positive stories about Africa in my discussions with others."

Over time, Ms. Ndakorerwa came to embrace her role as a bridge between the cultures. But, it wasn't until she moved to China that she grasped the dire need for a more positive narrative on Africa. "As I integrated further into German society, people could easily relate to me, but they still struggled to relate to Africa. I gradually came to see myself as a bridge. I made it a point to identify myself as a Rwandan and update their images of Africa. The urgent need for this role surfaced when I moved to China for college. While in Germany people tried to be discreet about their stereotypes, in China people were rather upfront about them. To many Chinese, Africa was just about war, poverty, and disease. At first, like many of my friends from other African countries in Hong Kong, I was horrified and deeply offended. But then I tried not to take the stereotypes personally and sought, instead, to understand the reasons behind them. I soon realized that, not unlike Germany, the stereotypes were rooted in an entrenched narrative of a hopeless Africa. A narrative propagated by the media and fueled by the limited interaction between Chinese and Africans. Building on my experience in Germany, I quickly integrated into Chinese society and began to break the monolithic narrative by sharing positive stories and getting my Chinese friends excited about Africa."

While Germany alerted her to the opportunity to serve as a bridge, and China underscored the imperative need to change Africa's narrative, the United States gave her confidence in her abilities to do so. "When I moved to the U.S. to pursue my master's studies as the Harambe Fletcher Scholar, I developed a friendship with a Japanese classmate. Towards the end of her first year at Fletcher, she confided in me that she had been offered an opportunity to work in Rwanda during the summer. She was inclined to turn it down because of Ebola and other concerns. At the time, there had been no reported cases of the virus in Rwanda, which was over 2,500 miles away from the nearest affected country. I think that because I had Japanese friends during my studies in China, I immediately understood why she was inclined to think that way. I knew that she simply had limited information and was basing her opinion on the indiscriminate reporting of the news media. I took the time to walk her through the facts. I made her aware that poor air travel connections within Africa meant she was more likely to catch the virus in London than in Kigali. Since she was interested in entrepreneurship, I also highlighted the growing entrepreneurial scene in the country. I am proud to say that as a result of our exchange, she got so excited about Rwanda that she accepted the offer and is now helping Rwandan entrepreneurs attract international investors."

Ms. Ndakorerwa's enduring optimism is also reflected in the choices of her academic and professional career. "When I was exploring college options, I consciously decided to attend school in Hong Kong. I felt that Hong Kong was a bridge between China and Africa, and since China was investing heavily across Africa, I sensed there was something I could learn. I chose to major in business because the more I reflected on how I could help outsiders perceive Africa as the land of opportunity, the more it became apparent that I had to study business. My underlying optimism about Africa has also shaped my career trajectory. At the end of my first year at Fletcher, I had two summer internship offers: one to work with a major company in Berlin, the other an opportunity with GSK in Rwanda. Career-wise, Berlin was the safer option. It would have limited my exposure to Africa, but it was a direct path to a stable career in Germany. GSK was more entrepreneurial in nature. The team in Rwanda was new and small, so the opportunity promised direct exposure to Rwanda but fewer clearly defined career paths. I deliberately chose GSK because I wanted to be on the ground and learn more about the Rwandan health-care sector. It was the right choice. Not only did I have the opportunity to manage strategic analysis as the Harambe GSK Fellow, but I also gained such insights into the country's health system that I eventually opted to add health economics to my studies at Fletcher. I saw so much promise and room for innovation that I just had to dig deeper and explore how I could add value."

In 2007 the Rwandan Development Board commissioned a study to identify the strengths of Rwanda's image. The findings were compiled in a publication entitled: *The Rwanda Brand Strategy*. The report's conclusion reads like a summary of Ms. Ndakorerwa's journey: *The single, defining characteristic that distinguishes Rwanda from other places is our Enduring Spirit. We have chosen hope over fear. We are united in our will to improve and progress.*

The excitement for Rwanda that the GSK managers experienced at the end of Ms. Ndakorerwa's presentation in June 2015, was not an accident. It was the result of Ms. Ndakorerwa's commitment to help shape the perception of the Continent by sharing her enduring optimism about Rwanda with the world. Her contribution is true to her own experience and reflects the plurality and diversity of efforts ultimately required to realize Africa's vast potential.

Ms. Ndakorerwa has grown passionate about the role health-care groups can play in the development of her Continent. "While telecom companies can help our people communicate faster" she observed, "health-care companies can keep us alive and productive." So as she embarks on the next chapter of her professional career, she is determined to continue to infect companies in the sector with her enduring optimism. "At the end of my studies at Fletcher in May 2015, I accepted an offer to work with a life science consulting firm. Based out of Boston, I will be working with the emerging markets team and intend to focus on health-care companies seeking to expand across African markets. This is who I am. This is what I want to do – just help others see Africa the way I do: a Continent full of hope, opportunity and contagious optimism."

CHAPTER III

Deliberate Audacity
Obinna Ukwuani, HEA '09

"We can no longer deprive our Continent of its own Thomas Edisons," asserted Mr. Obinna Ukwuani, HEA '09, standing in front of a fireplace at Harvard University inscribed with the Latin words *Alteri Seculo* – for the benefit of future generations. "These are the creative minds that could craft Africa-centric solutions – our own air conditioning systems, cars, and mobile phones. These are the innovators that could help us spawn an African industrial revolution."

Spellbound, members of the Harvard African Student Association gathered to welcome the eighth class of Harambeans to the Alliance, hung on every word of the towering and soft-spoken Harambean. "Just as Edison had his Menlo Park," Mr. Ukwuani intimated on the crisp spring evening of April 11, 2015, "so must we design the spaces where the young minds of Enugu State and the Continent at large, can be exposed to the technologies of our time and nurture their innovations into cutting edge factories and products."

The sheer audacity of his vision was not lost on the audience. "If our schools can't even teach basic math" posited a skeptic, "how will they manage complex engineering principles?"

Yet, Mr. Ukwuani's audacity mirrors that of his fellow Harambeans. Young African leaders bonded by their bold pledge, as signatories of the Harambe Bretton Woods Declaration: *to work together as one to unleash the potential of Africa's people, pursue the social, political and economic development of our Continent, and fulfill the dream of our generation.* These are individuals with an uncanny ability to imagine Africa beyond its present constraints, young innovators with the temerity to redesign the wheel in an attempt to circumvent poor road conditions in Malawi (Mr. Ngwenya); rebrand Africa by manufacturing high quality shoes in Ethiopia (Mr. Imende, HEA '12); and re-imagine education through mobile-based learning platforms (Ms. Rabana, HEA '14).

To the untrained eye, the boldness of the young Africans in our Alliance may come across as the fanciful machinations of untethered idealists. However, my work with Harambeans and my extensive interaction and interviews with Mr. Ukwuani over the years, lead me to conclude that their audacity is an informed and deliberate choice. A choice commensurate with their life experience and instrumental in overcoming the vicissitudes of the entrepreneurial process.

Makers Academy is the latest manifestation of Mr. Ukwuani's commitment to harness the transformative power of technology to unlock the potential of his people. Through the Academy, Mr. Ukwuani aims to provide a STEM-based (Science, Technology, Engineering and Mathematics) educational option to the over three million students in Nigeria's secondary school system. At an estimated cost of over $17 million, the residential, college-prep school will serve as a modern innovation space equipped with cutting edge design, fabrication machines and software to groom the next generation of African innovators.

A look at Mr. Ukwuani's journey reveals how an American-born Nigerian has grown so passionate about Nigeria and technology. Born in Washington, DC, on January 11, 1991, Mr. Obinna J. Ukwuani, is one of five children of two proud Nigerian parents. His parents immigrated to the United States in the 1980s thanks, in part, to a visa lottery program. While Mr. Ukwuani and his siblings were born over 5,000 miles away from Nigeria, the paterfamilias endeavored to ensure that his native Enugu State would never be far from the hearts and minds of his American-born children. "Dad spoke to us in his native language. To the point that even today, while my siblings and I cannot speak Igbo fluently, we all can understand it. He instilled in us a love for Enugu and would fly us back whenever he could afford it. He even had my sister and I move into his childhood home with our uncle to attend boarding school in Enugu for two years."

As Mr. Ukwuani reflects on his experience as a 12-year-old student in a boarding school in Enugu, it is apparent that his father's objective was achieved. "While many of my American-born-Nigerian friends did not associate with Nigeria and had only superficial ties to the country, those two years cemented my sense of Nigerian identity. I walked away with a nuanced understanding of the country and I developed a number of friendships that continue to this day."

While the influence of his father strengthened his bond to Nigeria, it was in the United States where Mr. Ukwuani first came in contact with technology. In 2006, he enrolled at McKinley Technology High School in Washington, DC. At McKinley, he became a member of an experimental class which was piloting the school's STEM-based curriculum. This opportunity equipped him with practical exposure to technology. He cloned DNA, grew bacteria, and tinkered with robotics. His academic achievements earned him admission into 21 of the 23 colleges of his choice. He opted to attend the Massachusetts Institute of Technology (MIT), where he continued to pursue his interest in the field.

But it was an experience with his cousin, Chidinma, that began to transform Mr. Ukwuani's interest in technology into a passion. In June 2011, at the conclusion of his first year at MIT, Mr. Ukwuani found himself typing furiously into a Dreamweaver sheet in the living room of his father's childhood home in Enugu. He was attempting to build a website using skills he had taught himself from an O'Reilly book on web design. After nearly two hours, with 75% of the website complete, Chidinma said, "Ok, stop. I now believe that you are a student at MIT."

Chidinma hadn't seen Mr. Ukwuani since he had completed his two years of boarding school in Enugu and returned to the U.S. to continue his studies at McKinley and the venerable MIT. Chidinma couldn't comprehend how his cousin had managed to make so much progress in such a short amount of time. How could the guy, who was one year his junior, and with whom he had spent countless hours in carefree conversations just a few years earlier, have mastered all these skills. In a candid moment of pure disillusion, Chidinma exclaimed, "It's simply not fair. Whatever we are doing in this country is simply not working. Our education system is ruining us. I've also gone to school. I've made the most of the opportunities given to me since your return to the U.S. Yet, I am so far behind, after only five years. It's simply not fair."

Chidinma's words struck a chord with Mr. Ukwuani. "At that moment, I realized that my practical exposure to technology at McKinley and MIT was at the heart of the growing disparity between my cousin and me. His gut-wrenching candor made me confront my observations about the stark inadequacies of the country's learning environment. I embraced my responsibility and vowed that I would do everything within my power to expose the *Chidinmas* of Nigeria to the opportunities that I'd been fortunate to have in the U.S. Never again would I let anyone feel the way Chidinma did that day."

That day also gave Mr. Ukwuani a profound insight into the power of exposure, an insight which continues to shape his thinking. "I came to understand that once you expose someone to something that is appreciably better than what they know, they can never again be satisfied with what they've known. For the rest of their lives they will be on a path to find that thing that you've exposed them to. I am now convinced that if you expose young minds to innovative ideas, their lives will be forever changed."

This was certainly the case for Chidinma. He was so impressed by his cousin's web design skills that two years after the living-room exchange he co-founded a tech company in Abuja. Today, among its services, the company provides web design for its clients – a skill which Chidinma learned from the same O'Reilly book Mr. Ukwuani had used just a few years earlier.

In 2012, Mr. Ukwuani began making good on his vow. Building

on his experience at McKinley and leveraging his network at MIT, he launched Exposure Robotics League (XRL), an intense summer program based in Lagos, which used instructors from MIT and a modified version of Carnegie Mellon's robotics curriculum, to teach students from across Nigeria how to program and manipulate robots. Each year, the five-week long residential program assembled a gender-balanced group of 30 to 40 students. To enable the participation of students from across the socioeconomic spectrum, Mr. Ukwuani raised over $350,000 from corporate groups to provide scholarships and ensure that every student had their own laptop.

In an attempt to overcome the inadequacies of Nigeria's rote-learning traditions, XRL's curriculum emphasized hands-on exposure. "We took a 30/70 approach. Students spent 30% of their time in lectures learning about programming and problem-solving principles, while 70% was spent in teams trying to get robots to autonomously perform a complex sequence of motions. One of the challenges required the students to write a program that would enable their robots to navigate an obstacle course, by keeping track of black lines drawn on the floor." XRL's approach was so effective, that even though the majority of students had no background in programming and a few had never even used a computer, "within three days" Mr. Ukwuani enthusiastically remarked, "every student was writing code."

To date, 113 *Chidinmas* from 17 Nigerian states have been exposed to technology through Exposure Robotics League. While his accomplishments with XRL have enabled him to begin to fulfill his vow, they have not given him the expected peace of mind – for XRL has alerted him to the enormity of the lost opportunity. "XRL made me realize that Chidinma is not alone. The kids that I met through the program were undeniably brilliant. I was struck by how quickly they absorbed the information and began to apply it to the realities around them. In our second year, I remember welcoming two exceptional students: one aspired to be a doctor, the other had an interest in agriculture. Midway through the program, they shared with me ideas they'd developed on how to use robots to perform medical surgeries and mechanize agriculture. Many of the ideas they suggested were already in use, but they simply had no idea. XRL was the first time they'd ever been exposed to programing and robotics. I was petrified. For a brief moment, I stared directly into the abysmal depth of the lost opportunity. I thought to myself: 'if this is what their young minds can envision after only a few weeks, imagine all the transformative ideas that a country of a 160 million people has already lost."

In 2014, Exposure Robotics League ceased operations. Its final report to supporters seems to suggest that in the face of the abysmal loss of opportunity, Mr. Ukwuani made another vow: *The Exposure Robotics brand is being retired in 2014. In its place, XRL's founder, Obinna Ukwuani, will launch Makers Academy…It will be a more mature and sustainable take on the Exposure Robotics concept, and will be a part of a much larger effort to standardize technology education in the Nigerian secondary school curriculum.*

As a poised Mr. Ukwuani embarks on the next phase of his bold vision, he is armed with the promise of the motto of our Alliance: *Audentes Fortuna Iuvat* – Fortune favors the bold. Like many of his fellow Harambeans, his experiences have taught him that sheer audacity can sometimes help overcome the paralyzing uncertainties of the entrepreneurial journey. "In my first year of college, I had a bit of an existential crisis and decided to take a short break from my studies at MIT. The short break eventually became a two-year hiatus. It was an unconventional choice with no certain outcome, but it was one I knew I had to make. Looking back it is safe to say that it paid off. During that time I joined Harambe, discovered economics, reconnected with Chidinma, and built the network and the confidence to launch Exposure Robotics League. Similarly, when it became imperative for me to travel back to Nigeria to make progress on XRL but I couldn't afford it, I shared the idea with a close family friend. To my pleasant surprise, he not only offered to fly me back to Nigeria but also to host me in his home while I conducted the feasibility study. I don't quite know how it works, but it is now clear to me that having the audacity to dream big can sometimes help you dare your dreams into existence."

It seems that Fortune is once again favoring Mr. Ukwuani's audacity, as he dares Makers Academy into existence. MIT's D-Lab and famed architecture firm, Mass Design, have lent their names to the initiative. The former CEO of Deutsche Telekom has joined his advisory board, and he has received generous offers of land and investment from prominent Nigerian figures. In a sign of his growing commitment, shortly after his formal graduation from MIT in June 2015, Mr. Ukwuani purchased a one-way ticket to fly back Nigeria.

Alteri Secolo, the Latin inscription above the fireplace at Harvard, is an excerpt of a longer passage in Cicero's *Tuscalan Disputations*. The complete passage reads: *He who plants trees labors for the benefit of future generations.* Only time will tell whether the sapling that Mr. Ukwuani planted on that crisp spring evening will blossom into his bold vision for Makers Academy. But my time with him and his fellow Harambeans assures me that Makers Academy is not simply a venture, but the manifestation of a core set of deeply-rooted values. Irrespective of the outcome of this most recent manifestation, I am confident that these values will endure and that Mr. Ukwuani will continue to labor for the benefit of future generations.

CHAPTER IV

Dream on a Piece of Paper
Journey of our Alliance

"Hitch your wagon to something larger than yourself."

Like the decisive whistle command of a seasoned drum major, these were the inspiring words that set in motion the journey of our *Dream on a Piece of Paper*, as we fondly refer to Harambe. Delivered by U.S. presidential candidate, Senator Barack Obama, at my college commencement on May 19, 2007, his words were a boost to my lifelong voyage to Harambe.

His message came at the conclusion of four formative years of personal and professional growth as a student at Southern New Hampshire University, a private college in New England. Years that whetted my appetite for direct engagement with the social issues of our time and taught me the chastening lessons of leadership.

Having arrived in New England from a five year odyssey into Ancient Greece and Rome, as a student of the classics at Julius Caesar Lyceum in Rome, Italy, I was determined to use my American experience to put into practice my observations on the evolution of Western Civilization.

So with great alacrity, I leapt at every opportunity to lead. I spearheaded campus efforts to celebrate the legacy of Rosa Parks and Dr. Martin Luther King. I raised funds and traveled to New Orleans to help the victims of Hurricane Katrina. I was elected the first black student-body president and leveraged the opportunity to support an initiative to equip rural schools in South Africa with desktop computers.

These experiences built my faith in the ability of a small group of committed people to improve their surroundings and awakened me to a moral obligation to act on the challenges afflicting communities in my proximity – the same urge for servant leadership that drove Mr. Williams from the classrooms of MIT to the Moringa fields of Ghana. In this context, the words of Senator Barack Obama struck me as a call to action, a challenge to deploy the lessons of my college experience to the world beyond the confines of the Ivory Tower.

As a descendant of the over 12 million Africans who were shipped to the Americas during the Transatlantic Slave Trade, my connections to Africa were purely ancestral. Born in Costa Rica, raised in Italy, and educated in the United States and Taiwan, my exposure to the challenges and opportunities of the Continent began in college. There I had an opportunity to work with Prince Soko, a proud Zimbabwean from whom I inherited an unwavering faith in the vast potential of Africa's youth – a faith which was strengthened by my interactions with other young Africans at conferences across the U.S.

These exchanges sensitized me to a generational yearn for bold action against the obstacles that stood in the way of Africa's prosperity – a desire that was accentuated in 2007 by Ghana's celebration of its 50th anniversary of independence. As Ghana was the first African country to gain independence, many openly wondered why after 50 years of self-governance, Ghana and the Continent at large were still home to some of the world's most indigent populations.

Nothing But a Dream on a Piece of Paper

Armed with Senator Obama's call to action, I stepped outside the comfort of my campus, intent on creating a vehicle that could channel the collective yearning for bold action of young African professionals. Along the way, a cadre of visionary young African leaders rallied around the idea, including Prince Soko, HEA '08, and Taf Mbanga, HEA '08, of Zimbabwe, Halima Hima, HEA '08, of Niger, Rosie Osire, HEA '08, of Kenya, Yonas Beshawred, HEA '08, of Ethiopia, Lanre Aina, HEA '08, of Nigeria and other founding members. Along with my college classmate, Brian Kanarek, and other supporters we fleshed out the idea and developed a shared vision.

Together, with an ambition that echoed Mr. Ukwuani's vision for Makers Academy, we devised a bold plan to jumpstart the Continent's development by traveling to ten African countries with a select group of young leaders, in an attempt to identify practical solutions that could be scaled across the length and breadth of Africa. In our youthful audacity we dubbed the effort, *Harambe Endeavor: The Sons and Daughters of Africa in Search of the Soul of Africa.*

With far more questions than answers, we launched our North-America-wide search for the *Sons and Daughters of Africa.* Guided by our conviction that if we could tap into Africa's greatest resource, its enterprising youth, we would in time find congruous answers.

Equipped with an extensive application, we crisscrossed the United States urging young African students to join our amorphous effort. But on September 23, 2007, it dawned on us just how fragile was our nascent endeavor. As I tendered the lengthy paper application to a passing student on the campus of the Massachusetts Institute of Technology (MIT), he respectfully accepted it and without the slightest semblance of interest, he simply walked away. In that instant, I realized that the paper, which embodied our bold dream, was of little value to the world. "Nothing but a dream on a piece of paper," I remarked, "that's all we have" – at the time, an unvarnished acknowledgment of the precariousness of the idea and the daunting task of convincing the world of its validity.

At the end of that dreadful day, in spite of our summer long efforts, not a single person had filled out an application. Battered and bruised we licked our wounds in a vain attempt for consolation. It was a disheartening blow that brought us to the brink of surrender.

In the depths of our inconsolable despair, we reminded ourselves of the stark needs of the people we were ultimately trying to serve. Parents who couldn't afford adequate educational opportunities for their children. Children who lost their parents to preventable diseases. Enterprising young Africans with limited opportunities. Individuals who would consider our bad day in America a true blessing. So, like a fish out of water in a hopeless spasm for oxygen, we decided to try again the next day.

As fate would have it, our fortunes turned on September 24, 2007. From 9 a.m. that morning until 2 a.m. of the following day, I spoke to groups of students who seemed suddenly infected with a contagious form of Harambe fever. It was a glorious day, which lives on in the mythology of our Alliance with the mnemonic catchline: *Remember, Remember the 24th of September.*

Of the hundreds of students we spoke to about joining Harambe in the fall 2007, 121 completed our admission process. A process so demanding that one of the 32 admitted applicants quipped that anyone who had completed it must have had "a deeply-rooted love for Africa." That love is what made a small group of 32 young Africans into a potent force – for each one of them had *chosen* to join Harambe. This deliberate choice is the basis for the high degree of trust and genuine collaboration that characterizes our Alliance and is the reason why today, after almost a decade since our first selection, the dedication required to join Harambe has not waned.

Harambe Bretton Woods Symposium

Once we had selected the candidates, we quickly realized that since our 32 *Sons and Daughters of Africa* were scattered across North America, we had to bring them together under one roof at least once before our ten-country tour.

The location needed to be as inspiring as the young leaders we had assembled and as grandiose as our vision for Africa. It was then that I reconnected with the historic Mount Washington Hotel – a pentelic white marvel, perched on a hill in the Bretton Woods Valley of Snow, under the majesty of snowcapped Mount Washington. The site, which seemed to echo John Winthrop's vision of a *Shining City upon a Hill*, was the ideal home for our bold endeavor. Built at the height of America's Gilded Age, as a summer refuge for the leading protagonists of the era, the Mount Washington Hotel sealed its place in history as the site of the Bretton Woods Conference of 1944, which led to the establishment of the World Bank and the International Monetary Fund.

Without a penny to our name and *a rickety idea in a turbulent sea of skepticism* we were assured that any attempts to secure the venue would be an exercise in futility. Undeterred, and with the enduring optimism that Ms. Ndakorerwa came to know in that classroom in Germany, we scheduled a meeting with the management of the property and shared our bold vision for the Harambe Bretton Woods Symposium (HBWS), the annual meeting of the Alliance, which we argued would in time emerge as a premier gathering of young African entrepreneurs.

We urged the management to support our incubation stage by providing us free access to the resort. At the end of the presentation, the general manager of the hotel told us that while he was very inspired, agreeing to our terms would have created "a major hole in our budget." Without quiver or hesitation I immediately replied: "that is not a hole, it's an investment."

After a week-long deliberation, and against all odds, the management consented to our proposal and afforded us complimentary use of their conference facilities and one overnight stay. It was a momentous achievement. As the first major investor in our *Dream on a Piece of Paper*, their support was a clear vote of confidence in our fledgling effort and began the steady trickle that has led to the cascade of prestigious partnerships, which continues to this day.

Over time, our profound gratitude morphed into steadfast loyalty towards a group, without whose initial support, our journey might not have even begun – a loyalty that explains why after all these years our annual gathering is still held in New Hampshire.

The boost of confidence had an immediate impact. As some of the selected candidates were traveling from as far as California, we sought to extend the gathering to at least two full days. Emboldened, we took our pitch to Dr. James Wright, then President of Dartmouth College. In spite of our tenuous connections to the Dartmouth community, Dr. Wright and his team graciously agreed to host the inaugural class of Harambeans on campus for one day.

Additional expenses still required us to raise $10,000. While we had managed to secure in-kind support, we had never obtained financial contributions. Yet, we were confident that with two months to go and an extensive network in New Hampshire, we could raise the extra funds.

A week away from the start of the inaugural HBWS we had not raised a single penny. A concerned friend organized a dinner to dissuade us from proceeding with the gathering. But we knew that a cancellation would deliver a deathblow to our fragile effort. So we continued to engage our New Hampshire network in a desperate attempt to steer clear of certain ruin. With 48 hours to go, as embers of our flame of hope began to dim, Lew Feldstein, then President of the New Hampshire Charitable Foundation, gave us the grant which forever rekindled our flame of hope and embedded in our Alliance an eternal sense of gratitude towards all those who've chosen to believe in our *Dream on a Piece of Paper*.

Harambe Bretton Woods Declaration

Thus, what at first seemed impossible, then improbable, in the end became inevitable. Between April 18–20, 2008, 32 enterprising young Africans gathered on the Ivy League campus of Dartmouth College and the historic Mount Washington Hotel for the Inaugural Harambe Bretton Woods Symposium.

My decade long study of history, alerted me to the significance of the occasion. So as the gathering drew near, I began to pen a document to capture the idealism and audacity of the moment. A solemn pledge that would commit us all to a shared set of values and serve as the guiding star of our long journey. Words, which I hoped, would unearth the enduring gems of truth in the garden of our transient euphoria.

I composed the first draft of the document, edited it in tandem with members of the inaugural class and together, drawing on a potpourri of ideas from history, we created the Harambe Bretton Woods Declaration:

There exists a large number of skilled, creative and innovative minds across the Continent – a talent pool of young adults, conscious of the painful lessons learned by preceding generations; grateful for the toils and sacrifices of the few; cognizant of the daunting challenges that face a Continent; yet, eager to take their turn at Africa's helm; determined to maximize the opportunities of our time; yearning for a peaceful and prosperous Africa.

We, therefore, sons and daughters of Africa, assembled in the Harambe Entrepreneur Alliance, with the assistance of those who have come before us and those who share our vision, publish and declare our intention to work together as one to unleash the potential of Africa's people, pursue the social, political and economic development of our Continent and fulfill the dream of our generation.

We believe in the unlimited power of ideas and the immediate need for action. We value the untapped potential of Africa and we sustain that our Continent's greatest resource is its people. Our mission is to empower a people, to inspire a nation and forge the destiny of a Continent.

We refuse to lose our knowledge that man's proper estate is an upright posture, an intransigent mind and a step that travels unlimited roads. We will not let our fire go out, spark by irreplaceable spark, in the hopeless swamps of the approximate, the not-quite, the not-yet, the not-at-all. We will not let the hero in our soul perish, in lonely frustration for the life our Continent deserves, but has never been able to reach. We will check our road and the nature of our battle. Yet in the end, the Africa our generation desires can be won, it exists, it is real, it is possible, it is ours.

Shortly after noon, on the hopeful spring day of April 19, 2008, in the Gold Room of the Mount Washington Hotel, where the Bretton Woods Agreements had been signed 64 years earlier, the 32 young African leaders in the inaugural class of our Alliance signed the Harambe Bretton Woods Declaration. Every hopeful spring since that day, our Alliance has returned to Mount Washington to welcome a new class of Harambeans and reaffirm our solemn pledge.

Today, the Declaration is what binds together the over 200 young African leaders in our Alliance to date. It represents the acceptance of our individual responsibility in the realization of Africa's potential. It is a personal pledge made not to Harambe, but to Africa. If decades from now Africa's potential is not achieved, the dream of a generation not fulfilled, Harambeans accept to share in the blame. Conscience, not courts, enforces its moral dictates. Commitments which Harambeans, as exemplified by the stories of Mrs. Mukam-Wandji, HEA '08, Ms. Ndakorerwa, HEA '10, Mr. Ukwuani, HEA '09, and Mr. Williams, HEA '14, strive to maintain through their individual efforts within organizations or their own ventures.

In a sign of the enduring significance of the Declaration, the highest recognition our Alliance can bestow upon a fellow Harambean bears the name of the room in which we sign our Declaration, the *Harambe Gold Room Award*.

A Glacial Winter, A Buoyant Spring

The lofty rhetoric of our hopeful spring was followed by the harsh realities of a sweltering summer. In spite of our eight-month-long fund-raising campaign, we failed to secure the funds necessary to make our ten-country tour a reality. It was a traumatic failure. One that put into question the foundations of our effort and made us wonder whether we had all been living a lie. "This is the end of a Harambe" were the whispers of a few Harambeans and the fear of all.

Perhaps, we thought, our critics were right. Perhaps our hopes were the "fanciful machinations of untethered idealists," our goals "divorced from basic reality," and our dream "a crumpled piece of paper destined for the dustbin of history."

As we grappled with our humiliating failure some Harambeans began to ponder the next steps. Though disheartened, Olivia Mukam, HEA '08, of Cameroon and Tola Sunmonu, HEA '08, of Nigeria argued that our Alliance was "never just about a trip." In this spirit they traveled back to their countries determined to implement the incubators that they had conceived in the discussions leading up to our ten-country tour. Thus, the entrepreneurship programs of Harambe Cameroon and Harambe Nigeria came into being.

Their admirable victories, however, could not assuage the pain of our ignominious defeat. Our sweltering summer soon gave way to a glacial winter of self-doubt, recrimination and disorientation, a period that lasted for the better part of four years. The internal confusion and lack of direction was not lost on the second and third classes of Harambeans whose feedback forms read "disorganized and rudderless Alliance."

Our glacial winter proved to be too long for members of the founding team, some of who understandably began to drift away. Even I quivered under the bitterly cold spell and wondered whether it was time to abandon what some skeptics called my "college pipe dream." The all-volunteer organization could still not support my basic needs. I slept on borrowed couches and ate at the mercy of concerned friends and family, who, in subtle and obvious ways, urged me to reconsider my full time commitment to Harambe. The situation came to a head when in 2009 I managed to raise the funds for the second Harambe Bretton Woods Symposium, yet my phone was cut off because I couldn't even afford to pay the phone bill. I had arranged for a bus to transport the group at the conclusion of the Symposium from Bretton Woods to Boston. Yet, I had no way to leave and no place to go. I sat in tears in the Sun Dining Room of our Mount Washington Hotel wondering why? Why continue to fight for a *Dream on a Piece of Paper* that was still of little value to the world? Why endure the opprobrium of defeat and the protestations of loved ones? Why attempt to support the entrepreneurial aspirations of strangers, who may never even thank me? At that moment, I recalled what had led me to Harambe: my desire to bring ideas to life, my college exposure to Dr. Martin Luther King and the Civil Rights Movement, my work with the victims of Hurricane Katrina in a devastated New Orleans, Senator Obama's urging to hitch our wagons to something larger than ourselves. Combined, my recollections helped put my challenges into perspective and reminded me that ultimately it was not about me. I asked myself the three poignant Harambe Questions: if not now, when? If not here, where? If not I, then who? It was a moment of great clarity, which finally revealed to me the true meaning of the wisdom of Dr. Martin Luther King: "Only when it is dark enough, can we see the stars."

I wish I could say that my tears in the Sun Dining Room were the final blizzard of our glacial winter. But in line with the experience of Mrs. Mukam-Wandji in Cameroon, Mr. Williams in Ghana and other Harambeans, there were many more storms to come. A few months later I found myself stranded on Christmas Day in Seoul, South Korea, with no way to leave and no place to go. Yet, this time I was not alone. Gradually a reinvigorated Dream Team began to form, which helped me weather the sustained storms of our glacial winter: our founding designer, Matthias Reichwald of Germany, our founding treasurer Robert MacPherson of the United States and our founding director of partnerships, Yonas Beshawred, HEA '08, of Ethiopia. In later years, more Harambeans joined the core, including Yvonne Kamau, HEA '12, of Kenya and Garikai Matambo, HEA '15, of Zimbabwe. A pan African and global coterie of individuals who reflected the transcendence and broad appeal of the call to action of our Declaration.

Together, we picked up the pieces of the Alliance and reconstructed our foundation. Staying true to the seminal insight of our Declaration that the Continent's greatest resource is its enterprising youth, we set out to build a rich and diverse ecosystem of opportunities to support the entrepreneurial aspirations of young African professionals. We established partnerships with prestigious universities and international corporations and developed Harambe scholarships, fellowships and a robust network of angel investors from around the world. To reflect our new strategy, we transitioned the name of the organization from Harambe Endeavor to the Harambe Entrepreneur Alliance. In the process we built a global and pan African brand of young African entrepreneurial leaders, who today are gaining the support and admiration of their peers, African governments, international media and even the Queen of England.

The success of our new strategy became apparent in 2012, when Obiageli Ezekwesili, a long-time supporter of Harambe and World Bank Africa Vice President, joined us in Bretton Woods to welcome to the Alliance the fifth class of Harambeans. In her reflection about the challenges of the new-venture-formation process she told the class, "Look no further than Harambe for lessons on the entrepreneurial journey. Acknowledge your failure, learn from your failure, celebrate your failure, but never stay with your failure."

Thus our long glacial winter led to a buoyant spring. A spring that strengthened the resiliency of our effort, tempered our unbridled optimism with meticulous preparation and rendered explicit our latent audacity. A spring that cemented the distinctive culture of professionalism and collaboration of our Alliance and reaffirmed our firm commitment to servant leadership.

As seasons go, our long glacial winter is unlikely to be our last. But through the challenges of the road ahead, I am confident that Harambeans will continue to be active participants in the realization of Africa's potential. We will do so with the enduring optimism, deliberate audacity and commitment to servant leadership forever enshrined in our Declaration. For we will always choose to believe that: *Yet in the end, the Africa our generation desires, can be won, it exists, it is real, it is possible, it is ours.*